Contents

Ants

1 Start by drawing two circles.

2 Draw in the large abdomen.

3 Draw in the legs.

you can do it!
Paint the ants brown and use a darker tone for the lines. Add splattered ink for the texture.

splat-a-fact
There are more than 12,000 known species of ants.

4 Draw in the face and add lines for the antennae.

5 Add lines to the abdomen.

4

5

Bee

1 Start by drawing the head and body.

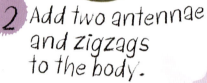

2 Add two antennae and zigzags to the body.

3 Add six legs.

Splat-a-fact
Bees make honey and beeswax.

You can do it!
Use felt-tip for the lines and add colour using coloured pencils.

4 Draw in the face.

5 Draw in four wings.

6

Mosquito

1 Start with the head and body.

2 Add the long abdomen.

3 Add the pointed feeding tube and the eyes.

4 Draw in six legs and add lines to the abdomen.

you can do it!
Use a felt-tip pen for the lines and add colour using fine liners. Use straight lines, squiggly lines and cross-hatching to add interest.

5 Draw in four wings.

9

Snail

Snails leave a trail of mucus as they move along.

1 Start with the head and long body.

2 Draw in a curly shell.

you can do it!

Use felt-tip for the lines and then add colour with watercolour paints. Dab on more colour with a sponge to add texture.

3 Draw in the face.

4 Draw in two antennae and add detail to the shell.

10

Beetle

1 Draw the body and head. The head is flat on one side.

2 Draw in six legs, each with two claws at the end.

you can do it!

Draw the outlines with a black felt-tip pen. Sponge on coloured inks.

splat-a-fact

Adult beetles have two sets of wings.

3 Draw in the eyes and a line down the body. Add two big mandibles (mouth parts).

12

13

Spider

1 Start by drawing the head and body.

2 Add two large fangs and the abdomen.

you can do it!

Use a soft pencil to draw in the lines. Add colour using watercolour paint.

splat-a-fact

Spiders are arachnids. They have 8 legs. Insects only have 6 legs.

3 Draw in the front four legs using curved lines.

4 Draw in the back four legs. Add dots for the eyes.

14

15

Dragonfly

1 Draw a body and a long abdomen.

2 Draw in the head and add six legs.

Splat- a fact
There are over 5,000 known species of dragonfly.

you can do it!
Use a felt-tip pen for the lines and a wax crayon for the detail. When you paint on top, the wax will act as a resistant.

3 Draw in two sets of wings.

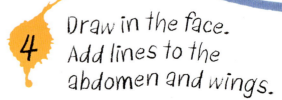

4 Draw in the face. Add lines to the abdomen and wings.

17

Caterpillar

1 Start by drawing lots of circles for the body.

2 Add two antennae and lots of legs.

you can do it!

Use felt-tips for the lines and colour in with wax crayons. Try different kinds of scribbly crayon marks to add variety. Paint over with a watercolour wash.

3 Draw in the face and add dots to the body.

Splat-a-fact

Caterpillars turn into butterflies or moths.

18

19

Scorpion

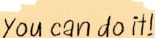

1 Start with the head and body.

2 Add the mouth parts and dots for the eyes.

3 Draw in the tail with a stinger at the end.

4 Draw in six legs using curved lines.

5 Draw in the front arms and claws.

21

Butterfly

1 Start by drawing in the body.

2 Draw in the face and and add antennae.

you can do it!

Use a blue felt-tip for the lines, then use wax crayons for colouring.

3 Draw in the wings.

4 Draw in the legs and add spots to the wings.

22

23

Moth

1 Cut out the wings and stick down.

2 Cut out six legs and stick down.

MAKE SURE AN ADULT HELPS YOU WHEN USING SCISSORS!

You can do it! Cut out the shapes from coloured paper and glue in place. Use a felt-tip for details.

Splat-a-fact Most moths like to fly at night.

3 Cut out and stick down the abdomen, body and head.

4 Cut out and stick down the antennae and chest. Draw in head details.

25

Ladybird

1 Draw the head and body.

2 Add a curved line to the body and draw in six legs.

3 Draw in the face and two antennae.

4 Draw spots on the body.

26

Grasshopper

1 Start with the head and the body.

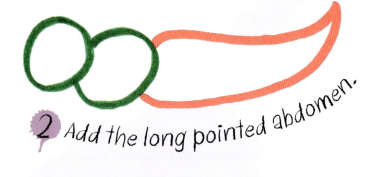

2 Add the long pointed abdomen.

3 Draw in the face, antennae and wings.

you can do it!

Use a felt-tip pen for the lines. Colour with pastels and blend them with your finger.

4 Draw in four front legs and two big back legs.

splat-a-fact

Grasshoppers make a noise by rubbing their legs against their wings.

29

Wasp

1 Start with the pointed head and the body.

2 Draw in the pointed, stripey abdomen.

you can do it!
Draw the lines with a felt-tip and stick down torn tissue paper for colour.

3 Add six legs and mandibles (mouth parts).

4 Draw in the face and two antennae.

5 Draw in four wings.

30

Index

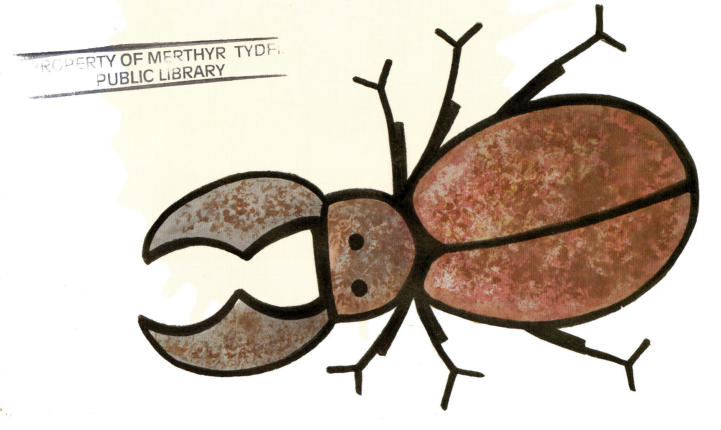